I0408257

Paranormal Investigator 1-5

PARANORMAL INVESTIGATORS, Volume 6

Rodney C. Cannon and Leo Hardy

Published by cannon books and media, 2016.

While every precaution has been taken in the preparation of this book, the publisher assumes no responsibility for errors or omissions, or for damages resulting from the use of the information contained herein.

PARANORMAL INVESTIGATOR 1-5

First edition. September 19, 2016.

Copyright © 2016 Rodney C. Cannon and Leo Hardy.

Written by Rodney C. Cannon and Leo Hardy.

PARANORMAL INVESTIGATORS - COLLECTION - BOOKS 1 -5

By.
Rodney C. Cannon and Leo Hardy

PART ONE

Paranormal Investigators One Ed and Lorraine Warren, The Enfield Poltergeist

Chapter One Between Movies and Reality

"Diabolical forces are formidable. These forces are eternal, and they exist today. The fairy tale is true. The devil exists. God exists. And for us, as people, our very destiny hinges upon which one we elect to follow." — Ed Warren

I arrived here almost the same way that most of you did. We saw a movie and we wanted to know more about the couple that inspired it. Before we really get started I would like to tell you a little something about myself. My background is as a screenwriter and as a micro budget film maker. I have harbored a love of stories about the supernatural since I was a child. It dates not only back to the movies that I saw as a child, but some encounters with the supernatural. Some would argue that whatever I heard or saw was the imagination of a small child, but most of those experiences were shared with other children in my family and even decades later we remember the events the same.

This book is not written to convince you about the existence of the supernatural either you believe or you do not. Just understand that before I begin that I believe in both good and evil. I believe in heaven and hell. I believe that not only people, but other things wander through our realm of existence and some of those other things mean us harm. If you need to place it in a more scientific context then I suppose that you can look at god and angels as positive forces and the devil, demons and evil itself as negative forces. Just as neutrons and electrons oppose each other.

This book is a short one for a reason. I wanted to touch upon a story and a few of the people involved. If you want to read the whole story you will find that Ed and Lorraine have written many books that focus on some of their more interesting cases. Also keep in mind that movies, no matter how well made, offer only a glimpse at the truth behind the events.

If you like this book, please remember to mention it to a friend and to leave a review. Thank you and god bless you.

Chapter Two Human Spirits and Evil Spirits

In the world of the paranormal, hauntings are very common occurrences. Individuals or families who have never before had any type of paranormal encounter - some who didn't even believe in such things - have suddenly found themselves the victims of terrifying ordeals brought about by dark spiritual forces.

Paranormal experts classify hauntings into two basic categories: human, or "ghost" hauntings, and demonic hauntings, generally those of a more sinister nature. Ghost hauntings are quite common. They are referred to as human hauntings because the common belief is that ghosts are the spirits of those who have died and who, for whatever reason, remain in the earthly realm. No one knows whether this is in fact what ghosts are, or if so why some of them choose to frighten and attack the living sometimes. It is possible that ghosts don't know they have passed on or they were not ready to go yet, so they remain earthbound as long as they can. Another possibility is that they may have unfinished business here and want to communicate this to someone still in the world of the living. It is quite possible that for the most part ghosts don't mean to frighten the living, but by their very nature, it happens. Still others may choose to haunt the living, enjoying the fear they instill. At this point there is simply no evidence as to why ghosts exist, what they are, and why they haunt the living.

Demonic hauntings on the other hand are identifiable by their vicious, evil, and harmful nature. The entities in these types of hauntings often hit, bite, scratch, burn, pinch, slap, or otherwise do physical harm to the victim. Whereas in ghostly hauntings the activities of the spirit are usually done surreptitiously and are rarely physically harmful, demonic hauntings can include victims being made physically ill, experiencing actual symptoms such as fever, vomiting, seizures, heart problems, fatigue, headaches, all unexplainable by medical means. A ghostly haunting can occur for rather benign reasons; demonic hauntings are never so. They occur with a sole purpose, and that is to harm or destroy the lives of the victims.

To date there is no scientific proof of either type of haunting, or the existence of a spirit world at all. However, for those who study these types of occurrences, and especially for those who have encountered them, there is no doubt that the spirit realm is very real and very active in the world of the living.

Chapter Three Spirit Boards more risk Than Reward

"Why do so few 'scientists' ever look at the evidence for telepathy, so called? Because they think, as a leading biologist, now dead, once said to me, that even if such a thing were true, scientists ought to band together to keep it suppressed and concealed. It would undo the uniformity of nature and all sorts of other things without which scientists cannot carry on their pursuits. . . ." — *Ed Warren, Graveyard*

The spirit board, also known as the Ouija board, has been popularly used since the time it was introduced on the commercial market in 1890 by a man named Elijah Bond. It has actually existed since ancient times in various forms. As far back as 540 B.C, mystic tables that were set on wheels were used in séances to contact dead spirits.

Elijah Bond marketed the board as a parlor game. According to some historians, when Mr. Bond attempted to get the patent for the game, the patent officer told him that he would first have to prove that it worked by having it spell out his own name, which was unknown to anyone in the room. When it did, the astonished officer gave him the patent.

The use of the board took off during the Great Depression, when it was used as a form of mystical family entertainment. It was also commonly used by spiritualists as a way to contact the dead and receive guidance. Today the Ouija board is seen as a harmless game that is even played by children. But is it harmless?

The Hidden Reality Behind the Spirit Board.

The use of spirit boards is actually a form of witchcraft. Whether or not the user is an innocent participant or an intentional diviner of spirits is unimportant. The same dark forces, evil spirits and demons are at work regardless.

An easy way to understand this is when a young child strikes a match. He may be unaware at the time of the power of what he has just done, but he is likely to get burned anyway. The spirit board is a portal or doorway into the world of the occult, where unseen dark forces are at work.

Witchcraft as a practice is condemned in the Bible, as seen in Deuteronomy 18, which lists several occult practices, including consulting with familiar spirits. To understand why, you must understand the nature of God, and the nature of the devil.

God and The Devil

We all know that God is the epitome of love. God created man because He loved him, but as early as creation the devil appeared, seeking to tempt man to disbelieve and disobey God. The devil is variously described in the Bible as a deceiver, one who tempts man to sin against God, one who causes turmoil and confusion, and even death.

Jesus gave a very clear definition of the purposes of God and the purposes of the devil, whom he called the thief. He said, "The thief comes only to steal and kill and destroy; I have come that they may have life, and have it to the full. (John 10:10, NIV)

It is important to realize that the devil will try to harm you if he can. He doesn't care whether you believe he exists or not.

What God asks of man in return for His love, care and protection is man's allegiance only to Him, as evidenced by the First Commandment. Witchcraft is condemned in the Bible because it seeks to obtain guidance not from God, but from other supernatural forces in the unseen world.

You do not have to try to contact a ghost in order to obtain guidance for your life. God has all the guidance you will ever need. All you have to do is call upon Him in prayer.

Avoid using such items as spirit boards or you may invite dangerous forces into your home and your life. The story of the Hodgson family is a case that should give all of us pause.

Chapter Four The Hodgson Family

"Mediums and spiritualists invoke powerful spirits or the souls of the dead, without realizing that they have given themselves body and soul to demonic powers. Even if it is not immediately evident, those powerful spirits always use their minions for destructive purposes.-
Gabriele Amorth Exorcist

The Hodgson family was made up of Peggy Hodgson and her four children two of which experienced what was deemed as poltergeist activity. Peggy called the police and claimed furniture had moved around the room unattended and that her daughters had been scared by ghostly sounds. Margaret, age 13, and her sister Janet, age 11, claimed they had seen and heard a ghost. They claimed they had been levitated around the room. Their story was found to be fraudulent by some who had discovered Janet banging a broomstick against the ceiling and hiding a tape recorder to give the illusion of poltergeist activity.

Later demonic voices had been heard in the neighborhood. Rocks and toys had been reported flying around outside. Overturned chairs and children suspended in midair had been reported. The story was covered in British newspapers the Daily Mail and the Daily Mirror.

On Halloween 2011, BBC News showed an interview with Graham Morris, a photographer, who claimed the events from 1977 were genuine.

Grosse and Playfair were two researchers who were members of the Society for Psychical Research that claimed the haunted house to be genuine. When Janet and Margaret admitted to their tricks to the reporters of the day, Playfair and Grosse convinced them to retract their revelations and hold to the original story. Janet had been accused of being a ventriloquist when strange voices were heard near her. These two investigators documented flying objects, bedclothes moving, pools of water appearing on the floor, ghostly apparitions, graffiti on walls, and spontaneous combustion. They witnessed a gruff male voice coming from each of the girls. Janet called herself "Bill" and described himself as an older man. These voices were recorded by BBC but upon later inspection the recording equipment was internally damaged.

Ed Warren, an American paranormal investigator, claimed to have seen Janet levitating while sleeping. He testified that the girls were the subject of demonic possession. Some believed that the girls were the puppets of a demon.

A photo of Janet in midair was disclaimed as a photo of her jumping on a bed. The adult Janet admitted years later that 2% of the claims had been faked. Joe Nickel, an unbelieving reporter, said that the number of hoaxes were closer to 100%. Nickel observed that the poltergeist acted only when no one was present.

These activities were supposedly happening in the years between 1977 and 1979 in a house in Brimsdown, Enfield, England. Professors of psychology Anita Gregory and John Beloff were never convinced of the authenticity of the girl's stories and concluded the girl's imagination was the only reality. Janet and Margaret still attest that the manifestations were real.

With so many taking both sides of this argument, the reader is left to his own deliberance.

Chapter Five The Paranormal Investigator

Paranormal investigators are people that look into the presence of supernatural beings such as ghosts, spirits and demons. Some people are skeptical about the work that these investigators do, because there is no scientific evidence that any of these beings actually exist. However, many people have found comfort from the reassurances that these investigators have been able to provide.

There are two main types of investigators, those that work in the field and those who do not. Some paranormal investigators will visit the property in question to carry out their investigative work. They will use a variety of equipment to detect whether there is a presence from a spirit or ghost. However, there are times when physical investigations such as these are not possible. This may be because the investigator has been asked to look into a case that is in a location that they are not physically able to get to. In these cases, they might use evidence such as witness statements to investigate the case.

Claims of supernatural activity have been made for thousands of years, and there have been people investigating these claims for the same amount of time. The profession of a paranormal investigator has come into the public eye in recent years due to the popularity of TV shows that follow investigators while they are working. This has led to people considering the possibility that supernatural happenings that can't be explained by science actually do occur on an almost daily basis, all over the world.

Chapter Six Paranormal Investigator Maurice Grosse

Maurice Grosse has made a living as a paranormal investigator. He was born in London in 1919 and lived in this country until he died in 2006. He was one of the most famous Enfield Poltergeists investigators that have ever lived.

Maurice received his education at the Regent Street Polytechnic which is located in London. He served in World War II as part of the royal army. His responsibility was to watch prisoners of war that were from Italy. He survived the war but tragedy in his life was far from over. He went home to his family and tragedy turned him onto the world of paranormal.

In 1976 Maurice experienced a great personal loss. His daughter was killed in a motorbike accident. After her death Maurice became interested in psychics and communicating with those that have passed on. He had a number of psychic experiences which caused him to join the Society for Psychical Research as well as the Ghost Club. Maurice was also a member of the Enfield Poltergeists club and spent hours reviewing evidence of encounters with those that have passed on. He is most well known for his work on the Enfield Poltergeist case. He is featured as a major character in the film The Conjuring 2.

Maurice became famous for his work. He appeared on a number of documentaries and gave details about his work. Even skeptics have found Maurice to be credible. He even dared people if they could convince him that his work was not accurate he would pay them a large sum of money. No one was able to prove that Maurice was tricking them. He was really able to communicate with the dead.

Maurice worked on many different cases and even became chairman of this organization. In addition to poltergeists he investigated precognitions as well as psychic photography. He continued to work in this field until the year 2006 when he died.

Chapter Seven Ed and Lorraine Warren

Anyone with an interest in the world of the paranormal will be well acquainted with the names Ed and Lorraine Warren. This husband and wife team are considered to be among the top experts on the spirit world, demonology in particular, in the United States. They are so well known for their expertise in the field and for successfully dealing with spiritual forces that for the past half-century they have been called upon by religious authorities to identify and vanquish spiritual phenomenon of a dark nature when priests or other church officials have come under attack.

Edward "Ed" Warren Miney and Lorraine Rita Moran met as teenagers in their hometown of Milford, Connecticut, where he worked as an usher at the local movie theater Lorraine and her friends frequented. Lorraine later revealed that at the moment she met Ed, she had a psychic revelation that this man was to be her future husband.

Lorraine was born on January 31, 1927. Ed was born on September 7, 1926. Ed served in the United States Navy during

WWII, then worked as a police officer prior to becoming an author, lecturer, and self-taught Demonologist. Lorraine's natural abilities as a light-trance medium and clairvoyant made it possible for the two to join forces and work together to become wildly successful paranormal investigators following their marriage on May 22, 1945.

During the early years of their marriage Ed attended Perry Art School, where he pursued his talent for drawing and painting. For a time they supported themselves and their newborn daughter by selling his paintings for the impressive sum of $3-$4 each. While selling his paintings and meeting many different people, if Ed got wind of any place that was rumored to be haunted, he would insist on Lorraine going along with him to check the place out. Ed had an interest in such things after growing up in a house in Bridgeport, Connecticut where a great deal of paranormal activity occurred. Lorraine, however, did not believe in ghosts. It was Ed's desire to investigate such places based on his own experiences in his childhood home that convinced her to go along with her husband on his excursions.

After experiencing firsthand the reality of the spirit world and its effects on the living, the Warrens founded The New England Society for Psychic Research. They had a true passion for the subject and a real desire to help people, both earthbound and those in the Spirit Realm.

Possibly the most famous of the many high-profile cases the Warrens worked on was the haunting of the Perron family of Harrisburg, Rhode Island in 1970. This famous haunting was the subject of the book,House of Darkness, House of Light written by Andrea Perron, one of the children who lived in the home and experienced the haunting firsthand. This case became the basis for the 2013 horror film, "The Conjuring".

Roger and Carolyn Perron and their five children moved into the home, known as the Old Arnold Estate, in the winter of 1970. The family immediately became the victims of vicious attacks by dark forces that filled the old farmhouse. Although every member of the family came under attack, Caroline seemed to draw the worst of the abuse. She repeatedly saw a female apparition which ordered her under threat of "death and gloom" to get out of the house. Through searching old records and photographs, the entity was identified as Bathsheba Thayer, a woman who had lived with her husband and three children near the property in the early 1800s. Bathsheba was rumored among locals to be a practitioner of the Dark Arts, a witch, and the fact that all three of her children all died at very young ages fed this belief. It was said she had sacrificed her daughter to Satan.

When the apparition's torment of Carolyn turned inward and she felt herself being possessed by the spirit of this evil woman, the Perron family contacted Ed and Lorraine Warren for help. Upon their arrival Lorraine immediately sensed a dark presence trying to possess Carolyn. She and Ed set about doing everything they could to dispel the evil presence in the home.

Despite the depiction in the film of the Warrens being able to cleanse the house of the dark presence that permeated it, the true story is that their efforts seemed only to aggravate the presence, which resulted in even more aggressive haunting. The Perrons were not financially able to sell the house and move away until 1980. Even so, the haunting continued after the family relocated to Georgia, though the incidents were reported to have become less violent once away from the Old Arnold Estate.

It is said that the Perron investigation and the events that took place throughout had a significantly detrimental impact on Lorraine Warren, both physically and emotionally. In 2006 Ed Warren passed away. Lorraine served as a consultant on the film 'The Conjuring', based on the Perron family haunting. Today she no longer takes part in paranormal investigations, but she continues to oversee the Occult Museum, a private museum located in Monroe, Connecticut, along with her son-in-law and the Director of the New England Society for Paranormal Research, Tony Spera. She continues to give interviews on a limited basis.

Chapter Eight The Enfield Poltergeist

The Enfield Poltergeist was a case of supernatural events being recorded and observed at a family home in the London suburb of Enfield. The family that lived at the house in question found it really difficult to live there, and their experiences convinced them that something dangerous as well as supernatural was taking place. It was a single parent family and times were not the easiest.

Unsure of what to do next the family asked for help and were sent Ed and Lorraine Warren to investigate what was happening to so adversely affect them. The Warrens were already known in the local area for investigating ghosts, claims of haunting, and spiritual events. What Ed and Lorraine Warren discovered provided evidence of events beyond the physical realm taking place.

The events that would later become infamous began during August of 1977. Divorcee Peggy Hudson lived in a council house in Enfield with her four children after the end of her marriage. Two of her daughters, who were then aged 11 and 13 respectively believed that the house was haunted, or had a demon or poltergeist infesting it. The Police were called out to the address after the first incident. The officer that went to the house saw some furniture move by itself yet could not explain why or how it was able to move without somebody moving it.

Once the tale of unexplained moving furniture spread the house became of interest to the media as well as people interested in finding out about the unexplained. The case attracted so much attention and people interested in paranormal and ghost activity were keen to visit the family and investigate what was going on within its walls. Those people that did visit the Hudson home would come up with various explanations as to the real course of events and if the causes were supernatural or could be scientifically explained. However they tended to want use any evidence to back their ideas about the events been genuinely paranormal, possibly even demonic in nature, or that things had been faked by the two girls with or without the knowledge of other family members. Those approaches meant that the evidence was not collected and used as well as it should have been.

However it was Ed and Lorraine Warren who convinced Peggy Hudson that not only could they explain what was happening in terms of what was wrong in the house, they could also find a solution to set the minds of the children at ease. The Warrens began the investigation with open minds, they did not have any preconceived ideas about events that had taken place and intended to gather as much as evidence as possible to support their eventual findings. The couple already had years of experience is leading such investigations, and would need all of it to deal with events they recorded and witnessed in Enfield.

The Warrens set out to record as much of the activities as they possibly could to gain enough evidence regarding any potential haunting, ghost, or demon presence at the home. They set up cameras and tape recorders to capture as much as possible, and to pick up things they may have been unable to hear or see themselves. Recording things also allowed them to play back film and tapes to check things in greater depth.

BOOK TWO

THE PARANORMAL INVESTIGATORS 2 AMITYVILLE AN ED AND LORRAINE WARREN FILE CHAPTER ONE 112 OCEAN AVENUE

If I had named this book 122 Ocean avenue how many of you would be reading it? You see that 112 Ocean avenue is the address of the Amityville house made famous in books and countless films.

Thanks to the recent hit horror film the Conjuring 2 there is new interest in the story of Amityville and what happened in that house.

Were the original murders supernaturally inspired?

Was the Lutz family tormented by a demonic force that made them flee their new home only 28 days after moving in?

What did the paranormal investigators Ed and Lorraine Warren believe happened in that house?

The job of a paranormal investigator is mostly to say no nothing is going on here. That there is a logical and natural reason for what has happened. Despite all of the famous investigations that we have heard and read about for ever place like the house in Amityville there are dozens that were dismissed as not having any supernatural activity within their walls. This particular story is unique and the dark forces encountered at 112 Ocean avenue is rare.

If you are ready we will begin with the brutal crime that introduced us to this house.

CHAPTER TWO RONALD JOSEPH DEFEO JR.

On Nov. 13, 1974, Ronald Joseph "Butch" DeFeo Jr., 23, committed a grisly crime that captured national attention. The quiet suburb community of Amityville, in Long Island, NY, was rocked by DeFeo's murder of his entire family with a .35 caliber rifle. The case attracted considerable media activity and even spawned the creation of a book and several movies. "The Amityville Horror," authored by Jay Anson and released in 1977, raised the possibility of paranormal entities inhabiting the house where the murders took place.

About the Crime

DeFeo stumbled into a local bar on the night of the incident, claiming that he believed someone had shot his parents, Ronald DeFeo Sr. and Louise DeFeo. He led several people back to his house at 112 Ocean Avenue, where they discovered that indeed his parents had been shot. Also dead were DeFeo's four siblings: Dawn, 18, Allison, 13, Marc, 12, and John Matthew, 9. The police were summoned, and they found all the victims lying face-down on their beds. The parents had been shot two times apiece while the kids were each shot a single time.

Ronald DeFeo initially claimed that a mafia hit man had carried out the executions, but detectives didn't buy it. They were troubled by glaring inconsistencies in his story and kept the pressure on DeFeo. He broke down the next day and confessed to the killings.

Trial and Sentencing

The case went to trial about a year after the murders. DeFeo plead insanity and claimed that he destroyed his family members because they were conspiring against him. Psychiatrists were called in by both the defense and the prosecution. The defendant was found guilty of six counts of second-degree murder, and he was given a sentence of six concurrent terms of 25 years to life.

Oddities About the Killings

It seems unlikely that all six victims would have remained in their bedrooms, lying on their beds, while the perpetrator moved around the house, firing his gun, but that's just what seemed to have happened. Strangely, the neighbors claimed to have heard nothing. No solid motive has been established for the crime although some have speculated that DeFeo did it to collect life insurance money.

Perhaps sensing that everything didn't really add up to a convincing narrative, Ronald DeFeo has made various claims over the years in an attempt to exonerate himself. He stated at various times that one of his sisters committed the homicides, that his sister and an unknown man did it and that he was guilty of the crimes but had help from friends. The authorities have paid him little heed because they consider his tales to be no more than fabrications as evidenced by their outlandishness and the frequency with which they changed.

The Amityville Horror Book

Shortly after Butch DeFeo's conviction, the Lutz family moved into the vacant house at 112 Ocean Avenue, which they purchased through a real estate agent. George Lutz, Kathy Lutz and their three children lasted less than a month in their new living quarters. They fled in terror, claiming that the house was possessed by malign forces.

"The Amityville Horror" by Jay Anson purports to be a true account of what the Lutz family witnessed during their residence in the house where the murders took place. Some of the weird items chronicled by Anson were:

•Strange voices coming from seemingly invisible persons•A hidden room within the building that wasn't on blueprints•Unusual odors with no natural causes•Unexplained damage to windows, doors and locks•Slime seeping out from the walls•Appearance and disappearance of bizarre auditory and visual stimuli

1. The Lutz family allegedly tried to get a Catholic priest to bless the house, but the ritual was interrupted or unsuccessful on multiple occasions. The priest began to suffer from stigmata and health problems. After 28 days, the family called it quits and moved out of the house. The details of their last night at the place were not told because they were supposedly "too frightening."

Public Response

Many criticized the book as being fanciful, unbelievable and clearly fictional. Nevertheless, it served as inspiration for more than a dozen films over the years. Paranormal investigators have looked at the house at 112 Ocean and have reached differing conclusions. Whatever the truth of the matter is, the horrible crime and the location where it took place have captured the public imagination. To this day, many people flock to visit the house whether out of a sense of morbid curiosity or a desire to witness fantastic, supernatural occurrences with their own eyes.

CHAPTER THREE HAUNTED AND EVIL HAUNTINGS

Why are some places considered evil? What do we know about places where things worse than ghosts haunt them, and people are murdered because of this? Is this really what's happening — demonic forces haunt a place and trespassers become susceptible to evil influence? Or are people experiencing echos from the past? A past where something so horrific happened that the emotions felt at the time created a tidal wave of energy that can be felt by others for decades afterward?

There's a credible theory that when something happens to people that makes them feel powerful emotions, an energetic "fingerprint" is left behind. It's said that this "fingerprint" is something that can be felt or experienced by others either in the form of ghosts, or in the form of paranormal activity such as doors closing themselves or frightening sounds coming out of nowhere. If this is true, it could explain millennial of ghost stories and tales of demonic possession.

Others believe that hauntings are the product of imagination. Groups of people will pass down legends from one generation to the next, the stories and myths evolving over years, becoming more believable to the listeners each time. Some say this is where superstition is born. Belief lends a tremendous amount of perceived reliability to the highly imaginative tales told by terrified people who set foot on forbidden ground. However this doesn't explain stories repeated by groups of people who all witnessed the same terrifying hauntings, or multiple individuals who experience paranormal phenomena in a place that nobody expected to be haunted. Perhaps the reason that phenomena like this have never been fully explained is that the hauntings are very real.

If you're open to the idea that paranormal phenomena can occur, it becomes a chicken and egg situation. Some places are considered evil. But which came first, the evil place or the evil people? Take the Amityville Horror for instance. When the Lutz family moved into the house 13 months after DeFeo ruthlessly murdered his family, they moved out abruptly. They said they'd been horribly terrorized by paranormal phenomena. A priest's hands were blistered. Voices ordered them to get out. Father Ralph J. Pecoraro was witness to all of this, and confirmed it himself in an interview. When one asks oneself if the Lutz family moved out because they were too disturbed about the knowledge of what had happened in that house's past and simply let their imagination run away with them, it's difficult to reconcile that with the fact that the priest probably didn't lie. But why did these terrible things occur? Was DeFeo possessed by a demon already present in the house? It begins to seem plausible when one reads the testimonials.

Was the house haunted? By who or what? Previous residents? Demons? Was there a "fingerprint" left behind by the rage of the killer and the blinding terror of the victims? Or was this something more terrifying than the human capacity to terrorize and kill: the presence of powerful demonic forces with the ability to control the actions of human beings? We may never know for sure.

CHAPTER FOUR THE LUTZ FAMILY'S 28 DAYS

On the night of November 13, 1974, a horrific tragedy struck the occupants of 112 Ocean Avenue in Amityville, New York. Twenty-three year old Ronald "Butch" DeFeo Jr shot and killed six family members; both his parents, two brothers and two sisters. All family members were murdered in their bedrooms of the home they occupied at 112 Ocean Avenue.

On July 4, 1975, George and Kathy Lutz were married. On December 18, 1975, the happy newly weds moved into the home at 112 Ocean Avenue along with Kathy's three children, Daniel, Christopher, and Missy. Due to the tragic events that had occurred thirteen months prior, a priest, Father Ralph Pecoraro, came to bless the house. While blessing the sewing room, Father Pecoraro experienced an unsettling and unexplained coldness on a lovely winter's day. As he sprinkled holy water, an evil, deep voice behind him told him to, "Get out!" The blessing of the house was terminated then. This began a series of unexplained, evil, possibly demonic events that occurred during the short period of time the Lutz' resided at 112 Ocean Avenue. A short time later, unexplained blisters appeared on the priest's hands.

During the short period of time the Lutz' called 112 Ocean Avenue, Amityville, NY home, many strange, peculiar, and truly scary events occurred that led them to believe the house was haunted at best, occupied by a demon at worst. On January 11, 1975, a mere twenty-eight days after moving in, the entire Lutz family fled the house and never returned. They left behind all of their belongings.

While living at 112 Ocean Avenue, youngest daughter, five year old Missy, developed an imaginary friend named Jodie. Jodie was a demonic creature that looked like a pig and had red, glowing eyes. On one occasion, December 25, 1975, George Lutz looked up at the Missy's window and saw a pig standing behind Missy. By the time he got up to her room, Missy was fast asleep, but her small rocking chair was still rocking back and forth. Another night, Missy said Jodie climbed out of her window. Kathy closed the window and saw red eyed glowing at her through the window. This evil entity presented itself to Missy in several other forms, changing at will. Among the forms chose, Jodie would often present herself to Missy as an angel. Was the house simply haunted or was there a demon residing in their home?

The Lutz family was haunted by eerie ominous sounds throughout their home. Bumps and thumps were heard all through the house; with no apparent cause. Locked doors and windows would open and close, but not by a human hand. Hundreds of flies would suddenly swarm the home from out of nowhere. Sickly odors would come out from nowhere. Kathy Lutz was beaten during her sleep by an unseen force, awaking with welts. One frightful night she was levitated off her bed. When the priest that attempted to bless the house tried to contact the family to warn them of the evil lurking in their home, sudden static sounds prevented him from getting the message through.

The Lutz family only lived at 112 Ocean Avenue in Amityville for twenty-eight days. During that short time period, the entire family experienced many horrific, unexplained incidences. We may never know who or what was in that house, but one thing is certain. The Lutz' house was haunted, possibly by an evil demon.

CHAPTER FIVE ED AND LORRAINE WARREN IN AMITYVILLE

In the early morning hours of November 13, 1974, a heinous event took place in a seemingly normal house at 112 Ocean Avenue in the upscale neighborhood of Amityville, New York. Twenty-three year old Ronald "Butch" DeFeo Jr., the oldest of the five children of Louise and Ronald DeFeo, murdered his entire family as they slept peacefully in their beds. Armed with a .35 caliber Marlin rifle, DeFeo first shot his parents to death before moving through the house to also shoot his two brothers and two sisters at point-blank range. All six murders took place in less than 15 minutes and somehow no one else in the neighborhood heard the gunshots and no one else in the home was woken up by the shots that were systematically killing their other family members. After murdering his family DeFeo showered, dressed, gathered his bloodstained clothing and the murder weapon and placed them into a pillowcase, then dumped the evidence in a storm drain as he drove to work at the car dealership owned by his grandfather where both he and his father were employed.

Throughout the work day DeFeo made a show of calling home and receiving no answer, commenting on it to his coworkers and wondering aloud why his father hadn't shown up for work that day. Upon returning home that evening, DeFeo pretended to have found his family murdered, running into a local bar screaming for help, claiming a break-in had occurred and someone had killed is whole family.

It didn't take investigators long to figure out what had really happened, especially after finding boxes of ammunition in DeFeo's bedroom that matched the murder weapon. The murders and subsequent arrest of the oldest son galvanized the community. The stories that followed soon gained international attention.

Though there was evidence of conflict between Ronald DeFeo Jr. and his father as well as admitted drug use by DeFeo Jr., he claimed to have been driven to kill his family by "demonic forces" that occupied the home at 112 Ocean Avenue. He said that these evil entities told him to kill them all. Ultimately, Ronald DeFeo Jr. was convicted of six counts of murder and sentenced to six consecutive life terms in prison.

Approximately 13 months later, George and Kathy Lutz and their three children moved into the home. They were aware of it's horrible recent history, but Kathy Lutz later said that this was not an issue for them, saying that "the DeFeo slayings weren't something that would bother us." The Lutzes were just happy to find a spacious house in such a good neighborhood for only $80,000. Little did they know that only 28 days later they would flee the house in terror, grabbing only a few of their belongings and heading for the safety of Kathy's mother's house close by.

Following their middle-of-the-night departure from their home, George and Kathy contacted Ed and Lorraine Warren with the help of a local television reporter who knew of their work in the field of the paranormal. Ed and Lorrain were a husband and wife team of paranormal investigators. Ed was a Demonologist and Lorraine was Clairvoyant. Both were devout Catholics. On February 24, 1976 the Warrens paid a visit to the home on 112 Ocean Avenue to investigate the claims of paranormal activity.

Immediately upon entering the house Ed Warren felt an "inhuman presence" so powerful that he said he felt as if he was "standing under a waterfall". He said it felt as if the presence was driving him down to the floor. He called upon the name of Jesus Christ and commanded the entity to reveal itself. He said that he knew then that it was no ghost they were dealing with, and no ordinary haunted house.

Lorraine Warren also sensed a demonic presence. She described her impressions of what she encountered in the house: "Whatever is here is, in my estimation, most definitely of a negative nature. It has nothing to do with anyone who has once walked the earth in human form. It is right from the bowels of the earth." It was the Warrens' opinion that the house could only be rid of it's evil entities by a "cleansing", a ritual performed by a Roman Catholic priest or an Anglican exorcist. George and Kathy Lutz had already had one negative experience with having a priest attempt to bless the house the day they moved in. They had asked a local priest, Father Ray Percoraro, to bless their new home. As he went from room to room during the blessing ritual, Father Percoraro was slapped. He also heard a disembodied voice say, "GET OUT!" Following his visit to the house he fell ill with flu-like symptoms, and his hands also began to inexplicably bleed. Based on this past experience, the Lutzes informed Ed and Lorraine that they would not be moving back into the house even if a cleansing ceremony was performed.

Although in the years to come there would be a great deal of speculation as to the validity of the Lutz's claims about the events that took place in the home, the Warrens never wavered in their convictions that the Amityville house was one of the most evil they ever investigated. They were even convinced that an evil entity from the house in Amityville had followed them home.

Ed Warren passed away in 2006. Lorraine Warren has stated adamantly that she would never so much as consider entering the Amityville house again. The Warrens believed that it is entirely possible that Ronald DeFeo Jr. was under the control of the dark forces that dwell in the house at 112 Ocean Avenue in Amityville, New York when he killed his entire family. Throughout their careers as paranormal investigators the Warrens saw many terrible things happen that were wither directly or indirectly attributed to demonic forces working through humans. Ed and Lorraine were both experts at recognizing such things and were extremely successful at driving them out in most cases. However, they were unable to deal with the evil that existed in Amityville, the evil that they fully believe cost the entire DeFeo family their lives, by murder and imprisonment for life.

BOOK THREE

PARANORMAL INVESTIGATORS 3 THE EXORCIST, FATHER GABRIELE AMORTH

CHAPTER ONE THE REALITY OF DEMONIC POSSESSION

I have never read horror, nor do I consider The Exorcist to be such, but rather as a suspenseful supernatural detective story, or paranormal police procedural. William Peter Blatty

Accounts of demonic possession predate recorded history. Tales of people being taken over and controlled by demonic forces have been told since the dawn of mankind. The Christian Bible even recounts stories of demonic possession (Matthew 12; Matthew 4; Mark 5). But is it truly possible to be possessed by a demon? Where does this belief come from? Is there any actual proof that possession is real? if so, how does one get rid of the demon?

Although most people in this day and age consider it to be a fictional concept invented by institutions of religion to frighten people into submission or by Hollywood to entertain moviegoers, demonic possession is treated as a very serious matter by the Church. In 1614 the Vatican issues a list of specific guidelines for performing exorcisms. This same set of guidelines was still in existence and was actually updated in 1999. Clearly the Church takes the subject of possession seriously. The Vatican even has a handful of fully-trained Exorcists on staff who are sent out to perform the rites of exorcism whenever a case of possession is brought to the attention of the Church which meets it's criteria: an aversion or physical reaction to holy water, super-human strength, speaking in unlearned or altogether unknown languages, and more.

A true demonic possession does not take place in a matter of hours or days as is generally portrayed in movies. Possession happens in stages: Manifestation, during which the contact between the demon and human is initially made. This stage of possession is non-invasive and leaves only a slight psychological impression on the individual; Infestation, which occurs when the entity begins to affect the individual in "outside" of his life in ways which call attention to its presence.

The next stage, Mounting, occurs when the individual begins to undergo mental and sometimes physical changes in order for the demon to accommodate itself. In a situation where the person is becoming possessed willfully, he will be able to "feel" the spirit entering his body at this stage. Riding is the next stage, when full possession occurs. The individual does not struggle against it.

The final stage is called Perfect Possession. This is actually a rare state to achieve. It occurs only after repeated possessions and involves the dark spirit and the person being possessed co-existing within the body, working together in all things.

An exorcism is only as effective as the individual's desire to be free of the demon. If the possession has progressed too far, it can be more difficult to exorcise the demon as the individual has become weak and dependent on the spirit. However, rites of exorcism performed by a truly devout and experienced Exorcist have proven to be the most effective way to rid one of an unwanted possession by an evil spirit.

The world may change from one era to the next, but spiritual warfare is as old as Creation itself and ultimately the power of spiritual good triumphs over the darkness of evil almost every time.

CHAPTER TWO THE HISTORY OF EXORCISM

"People shouldn't call for demons unless they really mean what they say."
—C.S Lewis

When most people think of exorcism, the first thing that comes to mind is a certain movie and a little girl with a head that spins backwards who does nasty things with pea soup and even nastier things with a crucifix. This is the Hollywood adaptation of a real-life case of possession and subsequent exorcism which took place in Maryland in 1949.

Robbie Mannheim was a happy, normal 13-year old boy who lived in Cottage City. Maryland. In 1948 Robbie's aunt taught him how to use a Ouija Board. A few weeks later the aunt died. Soon after her death, Robbie's family began experiencing paranormal occurrences in their home. Unexplained noises emanated from empty rooms, objects moved around on their own, scratching sounds could be heard throughout the house, etc.

The family thought that this activity was possibly the recently-deceased aunt attempting to make contact with them from beyond the grave; but when the incidents grew more intense and violent in nature, they realized something sinister was going on. When Robbie became the focal point of the diabolical activity and began acting and speaking differently, the local priest was called upon for help.

Almost immediately it was determined that Robbie was the victim of demonic possession. The priest and other Church authorities approved and sent by the Vatican spent six weeks performing the rites of exorcism over the boy. They were finally successful in driving out the evil entity, which claimed to be Satan himself, but at great cost to their personal health and well-being. Today Robbie Mannheim works for NASA and claims to have no recollection of any of these events.

Robbie's case is only one of thousands of examples of exorcisms performed in order to rid a human being of an invading evil spirit. Throughout history, exorcisms have been performed in nearly every culture all over the world, in a number of ways and for a number of reasons believed to be related to the presence of malevolent spirits.

In ancient Mesopotamia people believed all illnesses, mental and physical, were caused by evil spirits. Prayers and incantations were offered up to the gods against these spirits to drive them out and heal the afflicted person. In Persia around 600 BC, ancient records show evidence that rituals, prayers, and holy water were used by Zoroaster to conduct exorcisms. Zoroaster was a religious leader who is also considered to have been the first magician. He is credited with being the founder of Zoroastrianism, an ancient religion still practiced today.

The Christian Bible tells of Jesus Christ himself performing exorcisms, calling out and casting away demons who had possessed human beings. Jesus told his followers that they, too, had the power to cast out demons in the name of God. Christianity, like every other religion, has it's tenets and instructions dealing with demonic possession and how to perform exorcisms when it has been determined by the church that a true demonic possession exists. In modern times most religious institutions don't like to publicly discuss the subject, but with the current increase in cases of demonic possession and possession by evil spirits, exorcism has become a topic that is being brought more and more often into the light.

If exorcisms have been taking place in one form or another since the beginning of civilization, then there must be something to the practice. Centuries of these rituals, which are still being performed today, can't be wrong.

CHAPTER THREE
EXORCISM IN THE MAJOR RELIGIONS

-Yet I think the demon's target is not the possessed; it is us . . . the observers . . . every person in this house. And I think—-I think the point is to make us despair; to reject our own humanity, Damien: to see ourselves as ultimately bestial; as ultimately vile and putrescent; without dignity; ugly; unworthy. -William Peter Blatty

THE RITES OF EXORCISM AMONGST THE WORLD'S RELIGIONS

Exorcisms are a part of the entire world's religion which deals with the world of evil and demons. It's defined as the act of warding off or casting out demons or evil spirits from a person, place, or an object believed to be possessed. Various religions of the world perform the rites of exorcism in different ways and procedures.

Exorcism in Christianity Religion

The revised directions of performing an exorcism consist of a particular section from the Roman Ritual, a book that describes the official rites of the Roman Catholic Church.

To conduct the ritual;

- The priest or exorcist dresses in a purple stole and surplice.

-The rites mostly comprise of a series of prayers, appeals, and statements.

-The exorcist may take some actions at particular times during the ritual such as:

- Sprinkling holy water to everyone surrounding the subject
- Laying hands on the subject
- Making the sign of the cross on both the subject and himself
- Touching the subject with the Catholic relic (usually associated with a saint)

The series of prayers recited during an exorcism are broken down into two:

1) Imploring formula

It's where the priest asks God to free the subject from the evil spirits ("God, whose nature is eternally merciful and forgiving, receive our prayer that your servant, bound by the shackles of sin, may be forgiven by your loving-kindness").

2) Imperative formula

The exorcist demands in the name of God that the evil spirits leave the subject's body ("Depart, wicked one, leave, accursed one, depart with all your deceptions, for God has decreed that man should be his temple").

Though the Roman Catholicism is well known for its rites of exorcism, other Christian denominations also perform the exorcism ritual. Examples are:

- Anglicanism, the Church of England, has every diocese equipped with an exorcist.

-The Lutheran Church bases the exorcism ritual on the biblical declaration that Jesus expelled evil spirits with a single command.

Exorcism in Judaic Religion

The first allusion to exorcism surfaces in the Bible, in the story of David (I Samuel). In the New Testament, Jesus is said to have performed several exorcisms of demonic spirits in the first century. The book of Tobit gives a vivid description of the first exorcism. Josephus recounts events of exorcism in his Antiquities of Jews (2, 5, 8. 45-48).

He describes the procedure of exorcism as:

-the exorcist takes roots of herbs and burns them under the possessed person.

-surrounds the person with water and sometimes it involves immersing the person in the water.

Exorcism in the Islamic Religion

Muslims believe in the concept of a malicious demon. They hold that every individual is assigned a jinni, also called a hamzaad. The jinni whispers to people's souls so that they submit to evil desires.

Procedure followed during exorcism;

-The possessed person lies down.

-The exorcist puts a hand on the treated person and chants some verses from the Quran.

-Sometimes there is drinking of Holy water.

The exorcist recites particular verses from the Quran. The verses glorify Allah and invoke His help. Sometimes the ah-zan (the call for daily prayers) is also read; this has an impact of expelling the evil or the jinni.

The Islamic exorcism procedure is to recite the last three chapters of Quran (The Fidelity, The Dawn, and Mankind) and seek God's protection from evil.

The Takeaway

Performed to drive out evil spirits from a person, an object, or location; exorcism is universal religion practice. Though each religion has its own ways of performing the ritual, all of them have one single goal of expelling the evil spirits possessing a subject.

CHAPTER FOUR THE CHURCH AS PARANORMAL INVESTIGATOR

When a person is exhibiting odd behaviors people begin to worry. Some of these behaviors may not even seem human. If a person is speaking in a voice that is not their own and speak a language that no one has ever heard before there could be a serious problem. If this person has evil intentions they may be possessed by a demonic spirit. According to the Catholic believes this person may be in need of an exorcism. Before an exorcism takes place there are some things that the Catholic Church may need to do some paranormal investigating before this process begins.

There are some things that the Catholic Church will need to find out before suggesting an exorcism. There are some guidelines that must be followed. A person must be examined by a doctor to make sure they have no physical or mental health issues. In some cases these issues may be treated with modern medicine and this treatment will become more appropriate. This treatment needs to be tried first before an exorcism and shown to be ineffective. Before a full on exorcism some prayer can be used. A paranormal expert from the church will come in and address the situation. They will check out the situation and note if they feel a presence. Some exorcists from the church will be able to feel the demon spirit as soon as they walk into the home or come in contact with the person who is said to be possessed. If there is no reasonable explanation for the behavior it may be time to contact someone from the church to speak about an exorcism.

There are some signs that a demonic presence may have taken over a person. There are some things that a paranormal expert will look for to determine if a person has been possessed. If a person is not eating and has no appetite this may be a sign. This sign will go along with other signs including cutting or biting the skin, a feeling of coldness in the room, and unnatural body postures. If a person goes into a sudden rage and acts out of character it may be the sign of a demonic presence. If a person suddenly starts speaking a strange language especially one that is long forgotten such as Latin than this is a sign that they are not in control of their body. Violent reactions towards religious artifacts can be a sign that a demon is present. If a person has a violent reaction to something such as a cross or the Bible then it is time to call in someone from the church to investigate and help the situation.

If a person is possessed a Catholic Priest will come and help get rid of the demon. They have a special prayer and ritual for an exorcism to rid the body of the demon and bring the person back. It may take more than one exorcism to be successful. While the topic of an exorcism is still taboo to many there are many others within the Catholic religion that feel an exorcism is a real thing and is needed to keep the demons at bay.

CHAPTER FIVE THE EXORCIST GABRIELE AMORTH

- Be sober, be vigilant; because your adversary the devil, as a roaring lion, walketh about, seeking whom he may devour: 1st Peter 5:8

Many believe that exorcism is not real, that demon possession does not actually exist, and that exorcism is basically something that exists in the mind of Hollywood writers and producers. However, there are those who believe it actually does exist in real life, and who actually believe they possess the power to cast evil spirits out of people. One such person is Father Gabriele Amorth, the Roman Catholic Church's leading exorcist.

Who is Gabriele Amorth?

He was born in 1925 in Medina, Emilia. He was ordained a priest of the Catholic faith in 1954. He became an official exorcist in 1986. Over the years Father Medina has performed tens of thousands of exorcisms. By 2000, he reported as many as 50,000 exorcisms. By 2010 this number skyrocketed to at least 70, 000. By 2013, he had hit 160,000.

He is a member of the Society of Saint Paul, according to Wikipedia. This is the congregation founded by James Alberione in 1914.

He has also founded the International Association of Exorcists in 1990, and sat as its president until 2000, and remains honorary president until this day, at age 91, and will be until the day of his death.

Amorth's Advice to Those Wanting to Be Exorcists

It is Amorth's opinion that if you want to be an exorcist, you must be humble, have a life that's based on studying the Word, and on prayer. Also, you must be free of worldly concerns, such as money.

Also you must be a person of great faith. In addition, you must have a good reputation of being a man of prayer, charity, and good judgment.

Books He Has Authored

Father Gabriele Amorth has written two books, specifically on exorcism. The first of these was an Exorcist Tells His Story, and the other was An Exorcism: More Stories. These books were on exorcism as seen through the eyes of Amorth, an exorcist himself.

His Positions on Practices of the Day

Amorth has come out against the whole Harry Potter craze. He is of the opinion that anyone who allows his or her children to watch or take an interest in the series is allowing something that is satanic and harmful for the child. Because of this he has been criticized, especially throughout the non-exorcist clergy, as a bit excessive, one of those people who has allowed his profession to lead him to see Satan everywhere

He has similar views on yoga. He sees it as evil, especially due to its roots in Eastern religion. His critics have criticized him for speaking negatively about other faiths, seeing it as counterproductive.

His Basic Theological Beliefs

According to an excerpt from An Exorcism—More Stories,Amorth believes that Christ is the center of the universe. He believes that everything in it—the sun, the moon, the stars, and its people and animals, were all created for Him. He also believes that that the Christian would be remiss if he didn't at least acknowledge the existence of the kingdom of Satan, from which emanate the very demons he has been attempting to fight throughout his career.

Contrary to his critics that claim that he says that Satan is everywhere, he says, "No he's not. But when he's present, it is painful." He describes the Evil One as a bit of a chameleon who can change form, and speak different languages as well. One of the signs of his presence is the blasphemies coming from the mouth of the person he is possessing. So painfully real is Satan's presence that sometimes it takes a number of Amorth's assistants to hold down someone who is truly possessed of the Devil.

He has been asked by ABC News if the Devil can inhabit the Vatican. He said, "He resides there." He points to the child sex cases emanating from the Vatican as evidence, as well as the murder of his commander by a Swiss guard that took place there.

He is a firm believer in the Virgin Mary. Not just that she was the Mother of Jesus, but that She lives and breathes and still walks with us today and speaks to us too. He speaks of a time when She spoke to a seven year old girl named Jacinta, in Fatima, many years ago, and told her that the chief sin that is going to lead so many souls to Hell is sex sin, which She called "impurity", or the sin of the flesh.

He is, indeed, very theologically conservative when it comes to sexual relationships and the family. He believes, for instance, that divorce and abortion are a disaster. He has cited over 50 million children murdered by abortion. In other words, Amorth firmly believes life begins at conception.

Also, he does not speak well of divorce, euthanasia, or cohabitation, the practice of living together without the benefit of being married. His Views About International Events

It's his view that the emergence of ISIS, the organization known for its mass persecution of Christians, is a sign that we are living in the Last Times, the season that Christ spoke of that would be full of the signs of His imminent return. In recent years ISIS took over an Iraqi Christian town named Qaraqosh, causing the exodus of tens of thousands of people, mainly Christians seeking to get out of persecution's way. ISIS has persecuted and murdered

Christians, and people of other non-Muslim faiths in various parts of Syria and Iraq. His view is that this is clearly of Satan.

Putting It All Together

An exorcist for many years, Father Gabriel Amorth says that our biggest mistake is not believing in Satan, who has very dreadful yet real powers. He challenges us, even those who are non-Catholics—to reconsider such beliefs, and to think about Satan in terms of the many who have been delivered by Amorth and those like him. He wants us to consider what it says in the Bible when Jesus delivered people from demons—in terms of how the demons behaved; i.e. the blasphemies against God that would come out of their mouths.

Father Amorth is 90 years old. The time is very close when he will either retire or be taken from this world. However, his body of work will be left for a younger generation to study, like so many that have gone on before him.

References

lifesifenews.com/features/framorth_excerpt1_aug04.asp

abcnews.go.com/travel/chief_exorcist_rev_gabriele_amorth_d evil_vatican/story?id=100730110

www.catholicnewsagency.com/news/high-profile-rome-exorcist-isis-is-satan-31600

https://en.wikipedia.org/wiki/Gabriele_Amorth

BOOK FOUR

THE PARANORMAL INVESTIGATORS 4
THE BORLEY RECTORY, A HARRY PRICE FILE

CHAPTER ONE THE SPR

The Society for Psychical Research (SPR) is a parapsychological organization whose purpose is to research and understand occurrences of paranormal activity, reports of psychic individuals, and anything else under the paranormal umbrella. Parapsychology by definition is the scientific study of the ways organisms communicate and interact with one another and their surroundings in ways that are thus far not explainable using typical, existing scientific models. The SPR was founded in 1882, a few months after a fateful conversation between physicist William F. Barrett and journalist Edmund Rogers occurred in 1881. Its first president was Henry Sidgwick, and the organization's membership included numerous renowned individuals such as Arthur Conan Doyle.

The SPR, still active today, is unique among paranormal investigators because of their staunchly scientific approach. Rather than leap to the conclusion that all reports of paranormal activity and psychic phenomena are necessarily evil, always good or utterly and inherently false, they remain neutral and open to the possibility that parapsychological research has great merit. These aren't amateurs; SPR's trustees and officers generally hold multiple degrees, and the membership includes doctors, scientists, PHDs, and ordinary people. Since the membership is diverse, so are the multidisciplinary research methods. The academic background of the Trustees and Officers lends legitimacy and credibility to their work, especially when the SPR releases information about psychic and paranormal activity that would otherwise raise skepticism or even ridicule in the media and scientific community. It's safe to say that the Society for Psychical Research is a highly legitimate organization with a firm foundation whom have been successfully researching and documenting poltergeists, psychics and other paranormal activity for well over a century.

It's worth drawing special attention to Henry Sidgwick. He was noteworthy as a paranormal investigator because he was relentless in his exposure of fake mediums and fortune-tellers. However his practices allowed the people who likely had real capabilities to rise up to a place of higher respectability and furthered the understanding of what real psychic activity looks like. He's remembered by many as an esteemed researcher to this day.

The SPR's research about poltergeists is monumental. Innumerable accounts of poltergeists have been recorded and researched. The most notable — and the ones that helped to establish this activity as substantive — include cases where sounds can be recorded or where letters are written posthumously by the dead. One look up the SPR's recordings of the sounds that poltergeists make, and can see, when a computer generated visual is produced, how different the sounds made by a poltergeist versus the sounds made by the living are.

Also heavily researched by the SPR are unexplained lights and orbs, demonic possession, morphic resonance (transference of thoughts or ideas to other people) and mirror reading (commonly understood as crystal ball gazing). Of particular interest to many people are their reports on angelic beings, life after death experiences, and the appearance of deceased relatives. With their vast library of publications, one can get lost in the SPR's paranormal research archives for an eternity.

CHAPTER TWO THE BORLEY RECTORY A HAUNTED HISTORY

During ancient times, in the thirteenth century, a monk fell in love with a nun. They decided to run away and elope to build and establish a new life for themselves. While in the process if running away, before even embarking on this wonderful journey, their lives were cut short. While the monk was hung to death, the nun endured a worse fate. She was walled up inside the cold, brick monastery walls- while she was still alive.

Built on the site of the ancient monastery where the two lovers met their tragic demise, the Borley Rectory has become known as the most haunted house not only in England but in the entire UK. Despite warnings from locals that the site, commonly referred to as the "Nun's Walk", was haunted, Reverend Henry Bull built his rectory in 1863. Immediately, strange occurrences took place that gradually became stronger and more horrific with each new tenant.

This lasted until the fire that took the life of the Borley Rectory in 1938. Many believe the site is still haunted to this day.

In 1863, Reverend Henry Bull built the Borley Rectory and him and his family moved in. Almost immediately, they began seeing an apparition of a nun strolling along, roaming the property. The reverend was not fearful and thought this was entertaining. He built a summerhouse on the property so him and his son, Harry, could sit and watch the nun on her walk while they enjoyed after-dinner cigars. Guests, servants, the reverend himself, his son, and his four daughters all witnessed this phenomenon, as well as others. Other sightings at the time included the nun peering out the rectory windows.

When Reverend Henry Bull passed away, in the Blue Room of the Borley Rectory, his son inherited the home. The hauntings and sightings increased upon Henry's passing. In addition to the nun roaming the grounds, a ghostly horse drawn carriage was now seen racing around. During this period of time, the ghosts were peaceful. The only signs of ghosts were the appearance of the nun and horse drawn carriage, mysterious, unexplained footsteps, and strange creaking sounds.

After Harry Bull passed in 1927, Reverend Guy Smith became the new tenant of the Borley Rectory. The ghastly hauntings were too much for him to handle and he swift fully departed within one year. During the short period of time that the Smith's resided there, they called in famous ghost-hunter Harry Price. While visiting, Harry Price had a vase and stones thrown at him by unseen forces.

As the intensity of the terrifying hauntings, unexplained sightings, and strange occurrences worsened, reverend Lionel Foyster and his wife Marianne became the new tenants of the frightful Borley Rectory. The Foyster's would often become unexplainably locked out of rooms, their personal belongings would vanish without a trace, windows and other items would suddenly smash, and strange noises could be heard throughout the house. Writings asking Marianne for help would suddenly appear out of nowhere on the walls; some even as people stood and watched. The Foysters attempted to have the Borley Rectory exorcised, but to no avail. Marianne was thrown from her bed to the floor by unseen hands, and attacked by an unseen force. The Foysters logged and reported close to 2,000 horrific paranormal incidences to Harry Price before moving out in 1935.

The ghost hunter Harry Price leased the Borley Rectory next, for one year, to perform a deep investigation into these terrifying hauntings. He and his crew of investigators monitored and documented all of the fascinatingly terrifying events and ghastly activities that occurred. A séance was performed in which a spirit threatened the house would burn down that night and the bones of a nun's body would be found in the rubble.

After the one year lease was up, Captain Gregson moved in. His two dogs mysteriously disappeared and he was subjected to the same haunted circumstances as his previous tenants. Eleven months after moving into Borley Rectory, an oil lamp fell over, even mysteriously, or by Captain Gregson himself, and the building was burned to the ground. In 1943, a digging led by Harry Price uncovered the bones of a young woman. Harry Price gave the bone a real Christian burial, but the hauntings and strange occurrences at the eerie site continue to go on today.

CHAPTER THREE MEDIUM STELLA CRANSHAW

Stella Cranshaw, born Dorothy Stella Cranshaw in 1900, was a London born woman from the 20th century who wasn't exactly your average English girl. The daughter of a charcoal burner and a London nurse, Cranshaw boarded a train in 1923 where, by stroke of chance, she met Harry Price. This would be the beginning of her career as a psychic.

Harry Price, born 1881, was a British paranormal and haunting researcher of the early 1900s. He is most famous for his Borley Rectory investigation in which he lived in a purportedly haunted rectory building for a year and wrote his findings in a book he later published, giving the Borley Rectory the title of "most haunted house in England." In 1923 he, along with many of his contemporaries, were fascinated with finding a real medium or psychic. Price was getting tired of all the hoaxes and fakes in his search for a true medium. That's were Stella Cranshaw turned his luck.

While on the train, Cranshaw become bored and noticed Price had a stack of magazines in front of him. She asked to borrow a copy of the paranormal magazine, Light, and they had a long and fateful conversation. Over the course of the train ride, Cranshaw told Price about her several experiences with paranormal incidents. Among the phenomenon she experienced were cool breezes when all the windows were closed, unexplained flashes of light, and small objects floating without cause. Price believed she might be psychic and convinced her to participate in a series of séances to help his research.

Cranshaw ultimately took hand in three series of séances which each consisted of several sessions over the course of 6 years. These all took place in very controlled environments which Price labored over to ensure no fraud could take place. Several of Price's own inventions were used and he also brought in trusted colleagues to help with the sessions. None of Cranshaw's personal affects were allowed in the room, the furniture was set up in such a manner that actions could not be hidden from view, the room was locked and the key taken away, and Cranshaw's hands and feet were under the control of those in the room with her.

The first session took place in March of 1923 at the National Laboratory of Psychical Research. The second occurred on April 10th, 1926. Cranshaw's final séance was performed in 1928, after which she and Harry Price parted ways and she ceased to use her abilities. Cranshaw showed extreme physical and emotional exhaustion after her séances and her powers seemed to become less prominent as time went on. It is also possible that Cranshaw lost interest in or desire to use her abilities.

During the sessions Cranshaw and the others in the room experienced an array of events. There were often flashes of light, strange tapping sounds, and ominous levitation of smaller objects and even furniture. The temperature of the room often fluctuated toward cold during her episodes with cold breezes that at one point dropped the temperature from 63 to 43 degrees. During a singular session furniture being levitated was completely destroyed.

In her most powerful sessions, Cranshaw saw a being she stated was Palma. Many paranormal scholars believe this to be her spirit guide. Her most powerful and cited insight was when she claimed to see a newspaper with the name "Andrew Salt" written in bold letters on it. There was a falling boy on it that doctors kept pouring a white powder over. Over a month later a newspaper ad for Andrew's Liver Salt was printed on the front page featuring a picture of a boy who had knocked some salt off his plate. This was taken by many to be proof of premonition.

Given the great lengths Harry Price went to in order to ensure authenticity, many psychic researchers regard Stella Cranshaw as a true psychic and Price's reports on her to be a great resource. The reports still reside at the Harry Price Library at the University of London.

CHAPTER FOUR INVESTIGATING THE BORLEY RECTORY

Dubbed "Most Haunted Place In England" by journalists, paranormal researchers, and supernatural enthusiasts around the globe, the Borley Rectory is one of the most documented and notorious hot spots for paranormal activity. Although skeptics and critics alike, have had their reasons to dispute the alleged events that have taken place in this rural England locale, nearly 80 years' worth of chilling and unexplained phenomena has made it hard to sweep this story under the rug. The history of this eerie and mysterious place reads like a rap sheet of misfortune, begging the question of where did it all begin? Even before Harry Price, pioneer of the paranormal realm was summoned to take on the case, numerous reports of sightings and rumors of tragedy had been too overwhelming to ignore. The disturbing details uncovered in Harry Price's Borley Rectory Investigation have taken this controversial ghost story to legendary status. Adorned with stark peaks pointed to the sky like daggers, the Gothic style mansion lives up to its harrowing reputation. The timeline of historical events that took place at Borley Rectory set the scene, if not foreshadowed the trail of tragedy this notorious legacy has left behind. According to rumor, the land the rectory was built on was doomed long before its existence. Paranormal activity reports back all the way to the 13th century where a monastery was built prior to the rectory. A rumor that has been passed down generation to generation places blame for the paranormal mayhem on an illicit affair between a monk and a nun leading to their tragic death. The monk was executed, while the nun met a much worse fate; buried alive brick-by-brick. Some have even claimed a poltergeist tied to the land has been wreaking havoc since the Crusades. Since then, each successor has been met with a downward-spiraling slew of misfortune all the way until its demise during a fire in 1939. The deaths of two owners in the Blue Room of the rectory, alleged exorcisms, infidelity, and vanishing pets are just a handful of the copious amount of calamity that have occurred. Apparitions of headless horseman are commonly seen around the property. They are rumored to be the ghosts of the beheaded coachmen who tried to help the nun and her forbidden lover elope. The earliest sightings described have been of a nun roaming the gardens and then vanishing into thin air. The original builder and owner of the Borley Rectory Reverend Bull, built an addition to the house overlooking the gardens where sightings of the nun frequently appeared. Others have heard bells ringing, footsteps, and seen lights in windows when vacant. The large outcry from servants, spectators, and the Smith family who occupied the rectory at one point, lead to the local newspaper requesting Harry Price's expertise to evaluate the phenomena. Price wasn't new to the rectory when he returned for a second time to examine new, wilder claims he later referred to as "16 hours of thrills", made by the Foyster family. Marianne Foyster later admitted to fabricating the events that happened while they lived there to distract from an extra-marital affair she was having. Although her confession added to the disbelief of Price's credibility, the findings from his previous and subsequent journeys with other occupants long out-lived the doubts. Upon his first encounter with the rectory, immediate paranormal activity was strongly felt. He was met with various objects violently being thrown around the room and down staircases. Vases, candles, coin and rocks were seen flying throughout the estate. The daughter was thrown from her bed and almost suffocated by her mattress. The place remained vacant a few years before Harry Price took out a year- long lease to conduct an official investigation. During this time he placed an ad to recruit unbiased participants to stay for various amounts of time and record anything and everything they saw. Each were given an Ouija board and encouraged to use it. The events that took place during the investigation, including Price's creation of the ghost-hunting kit, have been both controversial and entrepreneurial for the field of Paranormal Research. One of the most chilling events that took place during this investigation was when a man named Mark Kerr-Pearse was eating alone inside of the rectory and was locked into the room. He first heard the turn of a key, and then much to his dismay realized it was being locked from inside, as he could see the key turning in the bolt by itself. During one of many séances conducted during his investigation, a bar of soap was said to have jumped into the air off the floor. Price mentioned in his writings that after the gardener and him chased after the ghost of the nun, a large pane of glass came crashing to their feet. Other participants have described the sound of a heavy dog panting over them while they slept. Perhaps the most significant of all the paranormal activity to take place, was a series of séances where contact with several spirits was made. The first spirit belonged to a nun who was murdered by her husband and buried within the property; her bones were purportedly excavated by price at a later date. Another spirit predicted that the rectory would fall victim to a fire, which it did less than a year later.

Despite the surmounting opposition to Price's work during the Borley Investigation, rumors of paranormal activity still lurk among the grounds where it once stood to this day. Generations of families who shared this creepy dwelling in common, have each contributed to the legacy that is still hot on the press. Nonetheless, throughout his work Harry Price has indubitably proven himself as a talented author, paranormal investigator, and a clever man.

CHAPTER FIVE HARRY PRICE PARANORMAL INVESTIGATOR

In the world the paranormal and psychics many people do not believe in the ability that a person can communicate with the dead. Other feel that there are selected people with a gift that allows them to be able to communicate with those that have past and see events that did not happen yet. While there are some frauds that give people with this gift a bad name no one can dispute the gift that was given to Harry Price. He was a British psychic researcher as well as author. He gained fame for exploring those fake Spiritualists and was an investigator into the phenomenon of psychics. One of his most famous paranormal investigations was the Borley Rectory in Essex, England that was said to be haunted.

Harry Price was born in 1881 in London. He attended school at the New Cross and later at the Haberdasher's Aske Hatchman Boys School. When he was a teenager he wrote a number of dramatic plays as well as some of the interactions he had with poltergeists as a child. Many of his plays took place in locations that were said to be haunted.

By 1908 Price was studying archaeology and got job working at a paper merchant. He also wrote for two papers in the Sussex area. Price became interested in the paranormal a joined a group called the Magic Circle. This group had an interesting in magic and conjuring. At this also sparked his interested in the investigation of paranormal activity. He worked with another psychic researcher named Eric Ding wall and learned about the fraudulent practices of those claiming to communicate with those that have past.

By 1920 Price has an interest in the paranormal that he could not deny. He became a member of the Society for Psychical Research and was able to point out a number of magicians and those said to be spirit medium that were fraudulently practicing in this area. One of his earliest research projects was in 1922 when he investigated William Hope who claimed to have the ability to photograph spirits. He exposed him as s fraud and was able to find out how he was producing the pictures of so called spirits. This was one of his first successes. Price went on to investigate a number of others. He has to learn all of these tricks. While many of these so called experts were good at their craft they were no match for Price and his investigative techniques.

By 1926 Price became well known in this area and his research he was able to form his own organization called the National Laboratory of Psychical Research. He tested a number of spirit mediums and was able to tell which ones were able to communicate with those that have pasted and which ones were making it up. He also found out the techniques on how a medium can fool the average person that is not educated in this field.

Price was offered a position at the University of London where he was part of the Department of Psychical Research. This department had the equipment he needed to conduct further research and educate others in this field. He also joined the Ghost Club and was a member until it closed in the year 1936.

Many experts in this field praised Price for his work. Richard Wiseman was another skeptic and he praised Price for being able to expose fraudulent mediums. Price was not only a skeptic but he was a scientist and had the knowledge and the research to study those that claimed to be blessed with the paranormal gift. Price was said to be one of the most fascinating figures in research and had methods that can be used by other investigators today. Price was said to pave the ways for other investigates including Ed and Lorraine Warren. These modern researchers use some of the techniques used by Price in order to debunk so of the modern mediums that claim to have the ability and the gift of communicating with the afterlife.

There are some famous mediums that Price was able to expose as being fakes. Eileen Garret was said to be able to make contact with the spirit world. Price invited her in to conduct a séance at his research center. She claimed she was able to make contact with the spirit of Herbert Carmichael Irwin. Two days after their meeting the R101 disaster happened. Some say the contact with the spirit world lead to this disaster. According to Price he was skeptical that Garret was really able to make contact with the spirit world. He said she was good at her craft but was a fraud. He also stated that she appeared to be in a trace and was convincing but her alleged contact had no effect and did not lead to this disaster. Some have even said that she had prior knowledge to the layout of the building where this incident happened and was able to repeat the information that she learned.

Price continued his research until the year 1948. He was at his home in Pulborough, West Sussex and suffered from a major heart attack. According to those close to him this heart attack almost instantly killed him. His widow gave some of his research to the University of London. This information including correspondence, drafts of his research that was not yet published, papers with libel cases, some of the reports on his investigations, and photographs. This information would be used to help other studying in this field and show them techniques on how to debunk mediums that are participating in fraudulent practices.

Price was a researcher that was before his time. He did not like people that were in a desperate time in their lives being taken advantage of those that were out to defraud them and take their money. While some people may have the gift to be a true medium there are others that are in the business of exploiting people. Price dedicated his life to conducting research to expose those who were in the business of fraud while establishing himself as one of the greatest paranormal investigators.

BOOK FIVE

THE PARANORMAL INVESTIGATOR 5
GAURAV TIWARI DEATH OF A GHOST HUNTER

By.
Leo Hardy and Rodney C. Cannon

CHAPTER ONE. THE INDIAN PARANORMAL SOCIETY

-The boundaries which divide Life from Death are at best shadowy and vague. Who shall say where the one ends, and where the other begins? - Edgar Allan Poe

With a population of over 1 billion people, India is one of the most densely populated countries in the world. This fact, along with it's location and long history of ancient spiritual practices guarantees that it is a land rich in paranormal activity. Even so, no serious, legitimate group dedicated to the study of paranormal activity existed in India until 2009, when Gaurav Tiwari founded the Indian Paranormal Society Tiwari had absolutely no interest nor belief in the paranormal whatsoever until an incident in 2003 changed his mind. He was in a hotel room in Florida when he encountered the apparition of a young girl. It was this event that made him a die-hard believer in the supernatural and led him to form the investigative group. He studied and became a certified paranormal investigator. He established the Indian Paranormal Society in order to educate the people of his country regarding matters of the paranormal and to help them to overcome their archaic, per-conceived notions regarding the spirit world.

The Indian Paranormal Society formed a research team called Ghost Research and Investigators of Paranormal (G.R.I.P.). This team investigated paranormal occurrences throughout India. Gaurav Tiwari was the team's lead investigator. As they conducted more and more investigations, their work became more widely known. Some people, particularly those who had been affected by some type of paranormal activity, believed wholeheartedly in the work that the Society was doing. Others, especially those who were older and who had deeply-rooted spiritual and religious beliefs, dismissed it.

Most of the Indian people considered the Indian Paranormal Society to be some sort of "modern nonsense", new to the country and not to be taken seriously. However, once the group began doing extensive, in-depth investigations and televising them the Society - and the subject of the paranormal in general - began to be taken seriously by the people of India. The public began to ask questions and to share their own personal experiences with the paranormal. As a result, the Indian Paranormal Society has grown in popularity, expanding their investigations all over the country.

Tragically, on July 7, 2016, Gaurav Tiwari was found unresponsive and mortally wounded in the bathroom of his home in India under very unusual circumstances. a thud was heard in the bathroom followed by the rattling of the door, as if someone was coming out. When Tiwari had not emerged after about an hour someone went to check on him. When he did not respond to three knocks on the door, guests in the home forced their way into the bathroom and discovered Tiwari on the floor, eyes bulging, gasping for breath. He was rushed to the hospital where he died before treatment of any kind could be administered. The only visible marking on Tiwari's body at the time of his death was a deep black mark on his neck. Ghost hunters and paranormal experts alike indicate that this type of mark is a sign of revenge by evil spirits in distress. To this day no exact cause of death for Tiwari has been identified in the matter.

The Indian Paranormal Society continues to operate and investigate supernatural incidents throughout India.

CHAPTER TWO The Dangers of Ghost Hunting

-We cannot banish dangers, but we can banish fears. We must not demean life by standing in awe of death. - David Sarnoff

On July 7, 2016, Gaurav Tiwari, founder and lead investigator of the Indian Paranormal Society died under very unusual circumstances. Guests in his home heard a thud come from a bathroom occupied by Tiwari, followed by the sounds of the door rattling as if someone were trying to open it, but it remained closed. After approximately an hour, a guest went to check on Tiwari. When he did not respond after three knocks on the door, guests broke the door down and discovered Tiwari unconscious on the floor, eyes bulging, gasping for breath. He was rushed to the hospital where he died a short time later. The only visible marking on his body at the time of his death was a deep black mark on his neck. Ghost hunters and paranormal experts alike agree that this type of mark denotes an act of revenge by evil spirits in distress. To date, no cause of death has been identified for Tiwari.

Those who are involved in investigating paranormal matters open themselves up to a number of dangers, spiritual, physical, and otherwise. In particular, those who are involved in ridding dwellings or people of unwanted spiritual activity or attachment are susceptible to often violent attacks from entities who are angry at their interference. Physical attacks are common. Investigators are often scratched, burned, bitten, hit, choked, etc, and in some cases the harm is much more severe, resulting in hospitalization or, in the most extreme cases, death.

Attacks can also come in the form of possession, with the spirit choosing to turn it's attentions on the investigator rather than the victim the investigator is attempting to help. When this happens, the investigator's entire family can be affected, as the entity can invade their home and become violent while working to possess it's new victim.

It is also common for spirits to attack the mental or physical health of the paranormal investigator. Many an investigator has been forced to give up their profession after becoming mentally or physically incapacitated due to spiritual attack.

For those who are skeptical about the world of the supernatural, these claims may seem less than valid. However, for those whose lives have been directly affected by entities from the Other Side, the dangers of being a ghost hunter are terrifyingly real.

CHAPTER THREE PARANORMAL BELIEFS IN INDIA

Introduction

There is a strong paranormal tradition in India. Almost all countries and cultures have their own ghost stories and their own convictions that there are evil spirits and malevolent supernatural beings. Supernatural beings and evil spirits are partly manifestations of insecurities that tend to be nearly universal to the human experience. However, these beliefs are more common and popular in some cultures. The modern world has made something of an uneasy and incomplete transition to rationalism. While many rationalists in India protest the persisting beliefs in the supernatural, paranormal beliefs still persist in many Indian cultures to this day.

Bhoot Ghosts

One interesting thing about a lot of superstitions and legends is that they tend to vary from city to city and not just from country to country. Talking about Indian superstitions is somewhat misleading, since some of them are really only popular in certain parts of the country. There are certainly Indian superstitions that are more popular across the country of course. However, many individual cities in India have their own ghosts. The belief in ghosts is particularly strong in India because according to Hindu tradition, it is not possible to destroy the soul. As such, the soul can return in many different ways.

The bhoot is a type of male ghost that a lot of people believe to be real in India. It uses black energy in order to taunt and haunt its descendants. There have actually been Bollywood films featuring the bhoot, which demonstrates the widespread popularity of this creature, even if not all Indians actually believe in it personally.

Bhoots are shape shifting ghosts. While they often appear in a human form, plenty of them also manifest as animals. They have backwards-facing feet, which is one of the ways that people can distinguish them as ghosts. They often appear in white clothing and specifically haunt the areas where they were killed. Bhoot spirits more or less bathe in milk, and it's believed that drinking milk that has been contaminated by bhoot spirits can lead to a demonic possession. Bhoot spirits supposedly also talk in a sort of nasal voice that manages to give them away, and this is one of the signs that people are supposed to look for when trying to identify a bhoot.

People can supposedly ward off bhoot ghosts using water or objects made from iron. Warding off evil spirits with water is fairly commonplace in superstitions. Burning turmeric is also supposed to get rid of them.

Other Ghosts

Pretas are other male ghosts, and they're specifically the ghosts of Hindu men who experienced violent deaths. Pretas are also created when their families don't observe the proper burial rituals. Essentially, they act as cautionary tales for families who want to forgo proper burial protocol.

The Hadal is a type of female goblin, demonstrating that there are ghosts and evil spirits of all genders in this canon. They specifically dig out buried bodies in cemeteries to use in their evil rituals. In that regard, they seem similar to necromancers and black magic practitioners.

There is also a female version of a bhoot called Achudail. This is a spirit that forms after a woman dies in pregnancy or in labor. Many of the features of achudail are similar to those of normal people, but they have been inverted in some way or another. Like bhoots, they have backwards-facing feet. Young men supposedly find chudail spirits at fields or road crossings. Generally speaking, loving achudail is supposedly fatal to the young man who loves her. However, some stories maintain that it is possible for a human man and achudail to marry.

Haunted and Portentous Trees

Given the rich plant life of India, it shouldn't surprise anyone to know that specific tree species are believed to be the favored habitats of certain malevolent beings. Many people believe that ghosts hide out in Peepul trees, and that it's a good idea to steer clear of them when it gets dark outside. Many people stay away from Banyan trees for the same reason.

Some people more or less believe that Sal trees can be used to detect the presence of witches. If a person writes the name of an alleged witch on the branch of a Sal tree, that branch will die. This belief is particularly strong in Jharkhand.

Possession

Many people in India actually report spiritual possessions. Exorcists have no trouble finding work when it comes to expelling evil spirits in India. Many of the evil spirits that they specifically try to get rid of are bhoot spirits, since it is often maintained that consuming bhoot contaminated milk can lead to a possession. The consumption of milk and dairy products is common in India, so it would follow that bhoot possessions would also be common.

Nocturnal Superstitions

The belief that bad things happen at night is found in almost all cultures. However, nighttime superstitions vary from culture to culture. In India, it's believed that sweeping the floor at night can cause bad luck. If nothing else, it's a good excuse to avoid doing chores.

Naturally, people are usually going to have to be particularly wary of almost all ghosts and other spirits at night. It seems that there are few that specifically prey on people during the day. People avoid all haunted sites at night, even though they typically avoid them during the day as well.

Conclusion

People might find that the belief in spirits in India is not all that different from what they might find in other places. There are certain elements in folklore that manage to appear over and over again. Paranormal and spiritual beings address humanity's fear of the dark, fear of death, and general fear of the unknown. However, the different ways in which those fears and concerns manifest can be interesting. The rationalists of the world and the rationalists of India might try to ward off these spirits in a different way, but even they might find the individual stories fascinating.

CHAPTER FOUR. THE LIFE AND DEATH OF GAURAV TIWARI

If you've followed the world of paranormal investigations, you'll know that the best ghost hunters are not plumbers or guys in tight tee shirts with spiky well-styled hair. The United States did seem to have cornered the market for ghost hunting shows until the arrival of Indian pilot turned metaphysical and scientific paranormal explorer Gaurav Tiwari.

Gaurav Tiwari was born on September 2, 1984, His family was Hindu and did not believe in spirits or ghostly phenomenon. The son of a successful family, he did some acting work at age 16 before going to the United States to train as a commercial pilot in 2007. As part of his training package, he was lodged in an apartment in Florida. This was a move that would challenge his former ideas as a skeptic. Soon things began happening that changed his mind about activity directed by those in the afterlife. Most notably, he witnessed stunning poltergeist activity in his apartment.

This spirit encounter led him on a path of paranormal exploration. He began studying the world of the metaphysical and earn certifications as a UFO Investigator and Lead Paranormal Investigator. Gaurav Tiwari earned the title of Reverend when he was ordained by the International Church of Metaphysical Humanism, http://www.metaphysicalhumanism.org/,

He came back to India trained as a pilot as well as a paranormal investigator, and looking for phenomena won out over pursuing a conventional career as a commercial pilot. Gaurav Tiwari founded the Indian Paranormal Society in 2009, which was the first ghost hunting society in India to use the scientific approach to distinguish spirit activity from naturally explainable phenomena. He also used his gifts to train as a hypnotist, which came in handy during paranormal investigations to help calm and center other participants.

Tiwari boldly went where others were afraid to go, namely the chiller slab in a morgue. During an investigation, one of his Australian team members got on the tray and then had to jump off due to fear. Tiwari who always wanted to analyze what he fears, or what other fear, he gladly hopped up on the table, and let them shut him in the locker, camera in hand. Although he was still on crutches from an injury, nothing slowed down his quest for knowledge and curiosity of the inexpiable.

Unlike other paranormal ghost hunting shows where the investigators act, or rather overact for the camera to display dramatic effect,Gaurav Tiwari retained his placid, professional demeanor whether he saw a full body apparition or visited the most frightening well-known areas of paranormal activity. He appeared on Haunted Weekends,Bhoot Aaya, and Fear Files, as well as many news programs around the globe, according to the India   Times,http://www.indiatimes.com/news/india/the-life-and-death-of-guarav-tiwari-the-ghost-hunter-who-ended-the-supremacy-of-supernatural-sadhus-258227.html.

One of his most challenging assignments was MTV Girls Night Out, where Tiwari and his team had three Indian female celebrities along to investigate a hostel. One of the girls, defined as a believer, got so scared that she couldn't speak, but Tiwari quickly, yet calmly removed her from the scary surroundings. On another investigation in Australia, one of the teammates had an irrational phobia of horses. As they were riding out on horseback to do the investigation, Tiwari refused to just leave him behind. He put his hypnosis skills to work and asked team member Ian to visualize two TV screens, one in black and white with his fears and one color television showing him without this fear. You can check out a clip of this and more of his best investigations on YouTube,https://www.youtube.com/watch?v=LbO8MIz_I7k.

Throughout his career, he participated in over 80 paranormal investigations, most times taking the lead. He awakened an interest in scientific investigation in India and became famous in his country as a metaphysical expert.

He wasn't afraid to debunk myths and hoaxes and used the scientific approach in all of his research. From the strange case of a worker who came back to her office after a holiday but had died 20 days earlier. to cases that he could rule out due to hysteria, hallucinations and other phenomena. He concentrated on verifiable data, such as electromagnetic fields, sound recordings, and temperature changes. He only alluded to something being "paranormal" if the phenomena defied all rational scientific explanation through rigorous testing. One of his most famous, and surprising debunking was the claim that Bhangarh Fort was haunted. His conclusions did not come up with any paranormal entities or energy at the investigation. This contradicts the claims of many who have had experiences visiting the historic fort, as well as mediums and Indian Spirit Doctors who have claimed the site to be haunted.

The strangest part of Gaurav Tiwari's life was his unexpected death on July 7, 2016. His wife said that despite rumors of marital problems between her and Gaurav, he was in good spirits. No one knew anything was wrong until they heard a noise coming from the bathroom. Upon opening the door, they found Gaurav Tiwari on the bathroom floor in his Delhi home with a black mark around his neck. Despite being rushed to the hospital and put on a ventilator to facilitate breathing, Mr. Tiwari could not be revived. Police say it was suicide or possibly homicide by a human; however, there are many who question these determinations. He was only 32 years old and his life revolved around his work and family. Tiwari was also a devoted yoga practitioner and woke every morning at 4:30 am. His family is heartbroken at his unexpected loss as well as fans that say the idea that his death was a suicide just doesn't add up. Gaurav had just signed a contract to begin filming a new paranormal show starting later that July, so why would he commit suicide weeks before the show was to start. When the family called a neighbor to break down the locked door after hearing no noise from the bathroom, Tiwari was alone. His fatherUday Tiwari said that he would never have killed himself and had just been married earlier in the year. He told the India Times,   http://www.indiatimes.com/news/india/the-life-and-death-of-guarav-tiwari-the-ghost-hunter-who-ended-the-supremacy-of-supernatural-sadhus-258227.html, that he could not commit further on his son's death, as it was still under investigation. Despite the lack of a conclusive theory on his death, various rumors appeared online. It is reported that one of his teammates from Haunting Australia, Allen Tiller, wrote a post on Facebook claiming that the cause was due to a sudden heart attack, which is unfounded in any medical diagnosis or fact. http://indiatoday.intoday.in/story/gaurav-tiwari-paranormal-investigator-foung-dead-mysteriously/1/712551.html.

Police questioned his wife and other family members due to rumors of marital strife and infidelity, suspecting it was perhaps a homicide. No further clues have come from those hours of questioning. Nothing on his mobile phone or e-mails suggested depression or despair. He posted on social media the day before he died and no reason for self-harm could be found. He was not suffering from any financial difficulties, according to many sources. There is some talk of an argument between him and his new wife because she was upset about his late night ghost hunting, but as that was his occupation, this doesn't seem like a serious problem that would lead to suicide or murder.

There are other possible reasons for his sudden demise, believers say. One odd clue was that from the inside of the bathroom, it sounded like someone had been struggling to turn the latch, according to First Post, http://www.firstpost.com/living/gaurav-tiwari-indian-ghost-busters-mysterious-death-is-magnet-for-paranormal-theories-2911340.html. Could it have been Gaurav Tiwari struggling with a malevolent force?

Some say that harmful spirit influences in Mr. Tiwari's life were indeed the factor that either murdered him or caused him to kill himself. Tiwari believed and taught about possible attacks from the spirit world that often left black or blue marks around the neck and other areas of the body. With his combination of spiritual training and scientific knowledge, he was a lifeline for people who felt they were under demonic or spiritual attack, although most of the time the problem the person was experiencing was emotional, not paranormal. For centuries, humans have had unexplained confrontations with the spirit world, leading to injury and sometimes death. It is said that Gaurav Tiwari had been battling a particularly nasty spirit or group of spirits that meant him harm. He had discussed feeling oppressed by a dark spirit, but his family, mostly skeptics, did not take this as meaning that his life was in any danger. On the contrary, he was described as being very involved in his work, but otherwise having an upbeat, yet driven personality.

According to an article in Indian Variety by Deepta Roy Chakaverti, titled "Why I suspect ghosts and demons are behind Gaurav Tiwari's death",http://www.dailyo.in/variety/gaurav-tiwari-bhangarh-fort-ghost-hunter-death-suicide-dark-spirits-rajasthan-haunted-spirits-ghosts-demons/story/1/11720.html, the famous ghost hunters death may be a case of one or more spirits from the 6,000 purportedly haunted sites he visited coming back at him, perhaps seeking revenge. She says that being in certain atmospheres can transfer negative energy, causing a person to become dark and gloomy. Such an example, according to Ms. Chakraverti, is Japan'sAokighara Forest near the base of Mt, Fuji, also known as "suicide forest" where the forest is the site of many suicides, mostly by hanging from the tall trees that inhabit the forest. Others have claimed that San Francisco's Golden Gate Bridge holds a dark appeal to the depressed to end their life. Perhaps, this author notes, the dark energy of Bhangarh Fort stayed hidden during Gaurav Tiwari's visit, only to attach to him and drive him to despair and eventually death. She has photographed orbs at the Fort and claims there is more there than meets the eye. The Bhangarh Fort is known to be inhabited by a wizard named Sindhiya, who in life asked a servant to obtain hair oil for the princess Ratnavati whom the wizard loved. The wizard infused the oil with a love potion to obtain ain the princess's affection. The maid spilled the hair oil on a rock so the wizard cursed the town and is said to still be looking for revenge. Ms. Chakaverti speculates that this haunted place, plus all the others he visited had an effect on his inner being and the energy piled up on him over his years of investigation, only to finally claim him in the end.

Whether you believe in the spirit world or are a total skeptic, one thing for certain is that Gaurav Tiwari made a name for himself by going places that others would avoid at all cost. Right before he died, Tiwari was featured on the cover of Youth Incorporated magazine,

No matter what his cause of death,Gaurav Tiwari made his mark in paranormal research and was responsible for a rise in interest in research and science-based ghost hunting in Asia. He lives on in videos, blog posts and in the hearts of everyone who was lucky enough to be on his team. For now, his branch of the Indian Paranormal Society, GRIP, is on hiatus in mourning for their beloved CEO. The Indian Paranormal Society's website,http://www.indianparanormalsociety.com/, has information about Rev. Tiwari's life and excerpts from his TED Talks, particularly one entitled "Ghosts Are People Too". You can find information about his 6,000 investigations plus the latest news about the society.

CHAPTER FIVE What We Know

Gaurav Tiwari, the 32-year-old paranormal expert and founder-CEO of the Indian Paranormal Society, dedicated his life to investigating bizarre and mysterious events, only to be struck down in death by equally unsettling circumstances. There are conflicting reports and disputed details surrounding the ghost hunter's death. According to family members, he returned home around 1:30 a.m. local time, following a late-night paranormal excursion. Then, he arose a few hours later to practice yoga and bathe. However, the events that followed leading up to his death are suspicious and could be fodder for the Indian Paranormal Society's investigation files.

Some of the family members present at the home claim to have heard signs of a struggle in the bathroom prior to finding Tiwar'sbody on the floor that morning. However, apparently, there was no immediate cause for concern until the famed paranormal expert did not emerge from the bathroom. According to reports, Tiwar's wife, Arya, became concerned after her husband failed to exit from the bathroom after an hour. When she attempted to knock on the door, she caught a glimpse of Tiwar's body on the bathroom floor and yelled for help.

Investigators became suspicious of the dark marks found around Tiwar's neck, which lead to an official cause of death of asphyxiation. However, several alternative theories were raised on social media and news reports. While some believe it was a case of auto erotic asphyxiation or possible suicide, others speculate that supernatural forces might have played a role in Tiwar's fate.

There is no denying that the world of the paranormal has its charms and enticements but it also has its pitfalls, especially when there is a morbid fascination or obsession with the dark science that Tiwar built his career and reputation on. In addition to his supernatural pursuits, Tiwar was also an actor, cartoonist, writer, singer, and ordained minister for Metaphysical Church of Humanistic Science (MCHS). Yet, the death of India's most famous paranormal investigator has all the earmarks of suspicious circumstances and could have been featured on his TV show, Bhoot Aaya, which focused on his supernatural endeavors.

WHAT WE KNOW

He was internationally popular in his field, and was featured on July month's cover of Youth Incorporated magazine. He seemed happy posting about it on his Facebook page a day before his death:

Gaurav's father told Times of India that Gaurav complained about some negative energy that was pulling him towards them. Gaurav's father said that his son told this to a daughter in law. However, she had chosen to ignore this.

A day before his death Tiwari was investigating a suspected haunted house in Delhi's Janakpuri area and returned home at around 1.30 a.m. at night.

Preliminary autopsy report suggested asphyxiation as the cause of death. A thin black line across his neck was discovered by the police at the time of death.

His wife, father and mother, were present at home at the time of the incident.

The official cause of death was posted as suicide. This could be the truth, but you will never find supernatural causes as the official cause of death ever anywhere. The only choices that someone who wishes to keep their job is going to be either homicide, suicide or natural causes. This death could have been something else. I leave you to come to your own conclusions.

Don't miss out!

Click the button below and you can sign up to receive emails whenever Rodney C. Cannon and Leo Hardy publishes a new book. There's no charge and no obligation.

Sign Me Up!

https://books2read.com/r/B-A-UOLD-ATZK

BOOKS 2 READ

Connecting independent readers to independent writers.

www.ingramcontent.com/pod-product-compliance
Lightning Source LLC
Chambersburg PA
CBHW062057280526
45788CB00003B/1261